Glyndŵr's Way

A Pocket Companion Guide

GLYNDÔWR'S WAY
A Pocket Companion Guide

Gillian Walker

Sketches and maps by George Allen

Management Update

© Gillian Walker 1990

First published in Great Britain 1990
by Management Update Ltd.
99a Underdale Road, Shrewsbury Shropshire SY2 5EE.
(Tel: 0743 232556)

ISBN 0 946679 39 8

British Library Cataloguing in Publication Data
Walker, Gillian
Glyndŵr's Way: a pocket companion guide.
  1. Powys. Visitors guide.
  I. Title
  914. 29504858

Management Update also publish 'Best Walks in the
Shropshire Hills' by the same author (Second revised edition
Summer 1989).

Typeset by Litho Link Ltd, Leighton, Welshpool, Powys, Wales.
Printed and bound by Billing & Son Ltd, Worcester.

CONTENTS

Introduction   1

Owain Glyndŵr — the Man   3

Glyndŵr's Way   9

     Maps   9
     Way-marking   9
     Navigation and Safety   10
     Animals   11
     Birds   13
     Flowers and Plants   15
     Trees   16
     Getting There (Coaches, Rail, Local Buses)   17
     Some Useful Addresses   19
     Local Information (Banks & Early Closing)   20
     A Final Word   21
     Glyndŵr's Way distances   23

Glyndŵr's Way — the Walk

     1. Knighton to Llancoch   25
     2. Llancoch to Felindre   27
     3. Felindre to Llanbadarn Fynydd   29
     4. Llanbadarn Fynydd to Abbey Cwmhir   32
     5. Abbey Cwmhir to Blaentrinant   35
     6. Blaentrinant to Llanidloes   37
     7. Llanidloes to Staylittle   39
     8. Staylittle to Aberhosan   43
     9. Aberhosan to Machynlleth   45
     10. Machynlleth to Cemmaes Road   47
     11. Cemmaes Road to Llanbrynmair   50
     12. Llanbrynmair to Llangadfan   53
     13. Llangadfan to Llanwddyn   55
     14. Llanwddyn to Dolanog   58
     15. Dolanog to Meifod   60
     16. Meifod to Welshpool   63
     Linking up with Offa's Dyke Path   67

Glossary of Words and Place Names   69

Acknowledgements and Further Reading   71

INTRODUCTION

Glyndŵr's Way or Ffordd Glyndŵr is a route for a walker to enjoy through central Wales. It is about 123 miles in length* starting in the town of Knighton in Powys and then crossing westward as far as Machynlleth before turning eastward again to Welshpool.

A circular trip may be devised by using the Offa's Dyke long distance footpath from Welshpool to Knighton adding another 26 miles. For the most part, the route takes the existing public footpaths, public bridleways and highways although there are sections which traverse lonely moorland and where, even if the public footpaths exist on the map, they are not often apparent on the ground.

The route originally was the 'brainchild' of Powys County Council in 1977: they have since carried out way-markings and maintenance of the public footpaths, stiles and footbridges. However, there is the possibility that with the aid of the Countryside Commission the route may be designated a 'National Trail'. If this happens, there may be alterations from the route now described and originally planned by Powys County Council. Whilst a decision is awaited on this, the County Council is naturally loath to spend much public money on anything other than essential repair and maintenance. Consequently, although the way-marking in certain sections is excellent, you will find it virtually non-existent in other areas. Do not expect to be 'molly coddled' with way-marks as on Offa's Dyke footpath or certain English long distance footpaths. If you should come across a serious obstruction on an existing public right of way whilst walking the path, then no doubt you will report it to the County Council.

* *By comparison the Pennine Way covers about 250 miles, Offa's Dyke Path 177 miles and the Cleveland Way approximately 93 miles.*

You will not find on this walk the high mountains of Snowdonia, the English Lake District or Scotland, but there is a lot of wild Wales between Knighton, Machynlleth and Welshpool. On good days when visibility is clear and you can see the mountains of the North and the South to either side of you, your exhilaration will be immense. On bad days when the rain is hitting you horizontally and when you are stumbling over tussocks and battling through the rainfilled drainage channels of the Forestry Commission you will be less enchanted. You will still be going through an area which at the moment is 'secret Wales' and you will be surprised if you pass more than one or two walkers on the whole of your journey.

On your way, the past is ever present. At nearly every turn there is some reminder of human-kind's previous toil, strife or happiness; nearly every ridge and cwm has seen a fight for survival, be it against invaders from the East with arrow or spear or invaders from the East with bulldozers and blue-prints for reservoirs, pipelines or ranks of Sitka. The very stones beneath your feet form part of the oldest rock to be found anywhere in the world.

This small country has one quality which is unique, namely its light. By the end of your walk you will have noticed that the trick of Welsh light is to make everything appear further away and higher than it actually is. This is a phenomenon which I have not witnessed in any other area and which manifests itself time after time in Wales. See if you can spot it.

Frustrating, tiring, wet, boggy, puzzling, exhilarating, interesting, all these adjectives can be applied to this route, but boring is not one of them!

Although named after the early 15th. C. warrior statesman, Owain Glyndŵr who tried to establish an independent Welsh Nation, the route of the Way itself does not noticeably pass by any major land marks made famous by Glyndŵr himself apart from Machynlleth town where he established the first Welsh Parliament. However, you traverse Mid-Wales along this route in the knowledge that the whole land was the subject of his nationalist fervour and one bit of Wales cannot be separated from another when it comes to the prospect of the wholeness of the Welsh nation.

OWAIN GLYNDŴR
— the Man

There is little detailed information about the early years of
Owain Glyndŵr though it is known that he was born in the
village of Glyndyfrdwy (now on the A5 between Llangollen and
Corwen) about the year 1359 of part-Tudor descent and into a
fairly well-to-do household whose parents owned two estates in
the area. He was a direct descendant of the Princes of Powys
and Deheubarth. He studied law in London and perhaps spent
as many as seven years in the London Inns of Court. To 'finish'
him as a young man he had military training as a squire to the
Earl of Arundel and later to Henry Bolingbroke. The practise of
the law brought him in touch with Margaret Hanmer, a
daughter of a judge of the King's Bench and of an Anglo-Welsh
family. The pair had at least two sons and possibly three and at
least seven daughters. His early country home was at Sycharth
on the other side of the Berwyns from Glyndyfrdwy towards the
Tanat Valley, one of the two estates of his parents.
In order to understand the reason for 'this man of his time' it is
best to realise that Wales was ready for change; drastic change,
in 1400. Life for the Welsh was becoming more and more
difficult under Henry IV and Nature — in the form of the Black
Death — had also taken its toll. The poor were becoming more
and more oppressed; the time was right for a sign to lift them
from their despond.

A quarrel with Lord Grey of Ruthin sparked the uprising which
caught the imagination of the nation. Grey, a member of
Henry's Council and a major landowner had taken some of
Owain's land at Glyndyfrdwy. Owain peaceably went to law
over it. His lawsuit came before the English Parliament in 1400
but he found little sympathy there, the attitude being 'what care
we for the barefoot Welsh dogs?' and his claim failed.

This was too much for proud Owain who had also been accused of treason. Having tried lawful means and failed, the warrior in him now took over. On 16th September 1400 with family and friends gathered around he raised his standard — a gold dragon — and was proclaimed Prince of Wales. Two days later his first battle for Welsh Independence took place at Ruthin against Lord Grey. His countrymen and women rallied to him and the nation was at war. Owain moved quickly sacking Denbigh, Flint, Hawarden, Oswestry and Rhuddlan but on his way to take Welshpool he lost against a force from Shropshire, Staffordshire & Warwickshire in a battle on the banks of the Vyrnwy. Owain's band retreated into the hills. Gwilym and Rhys Tudor, Owain's cousins, rebelled in Anglesey. Henry IV's men marched on, routing the Welsh along the way and returning to Shrewsbury by mid-October. Henry was in no doubt that the little rebellion was over. Henry IV was determined to put any Welsh rising down and is said to have executed Goronwy ap Tudor at Shrewsbury in September 1400 and granted Glyndŵr's manor and lands to John Beaufort, Earl of Somerset, although he could not gain possession because Glyndŵr held much of North Wales.

Henry IV then made matters worse by allowing the English Parliament to enact laws that were even harsher on the Welsh. The Marcher Lords were allowed to take any land they could hold which meant frequent and vicious skirmishes along the borders and mounting hatred by the Welsh for the indignities heaped upon them. His Parliament decided that no Welsh person could marry an English man or woman or hold official office and that the Welsh could not live in England and must pay for any damage done to English land and property in Owain's rebellion. Henry IV's harsh laws against the Welsh were designed to enforce English supremacy and put the Welsh in 'their place'. They went so far as to decree that 'Englishmen were not to be convicted by Welshmen in Wales' and that 'all castles and walled towns were to be garrisoned by Englishmen'.

Owain established a lair on land which is now beneath the water of the Nantymoch Reservoir. Abbey Cwmhir was looted and burned as the monks were suspected of having English sympathies. Welshpool was again attacked but resisted: his band returned back to his hideout at Nantymoch.

Henry IV had encouraged a large immigrant population from Flanders in South-West Wales who gradually spread out, but in doing so made themselves unpopular with the locals. They decided to march North and surrounded Owain at Hyddgen in the foothills of Pumlumon. Owain's band fought hard and desperately and the Flemish force lost several hundred men. This was a first real battle victory for the Welsh and the old fervour behind Owain was renewed.

On Good Friday in 1401, Conway Castle was taken by Glyndŵr's forces. Sir Henry Percy — 'Harry Hotspur' — had been appointed by Henry IV to quell the Welsh but when he began to realise that this was something more than local skirmishing he pulled his men out and returned to Northumberland. Later in the same year, Henry despoiled the Abbey at Strata Florida.

In 1402, Owain defeated the English at Bryn Glas near Knighton and captured his arch-enemy, Lord Grey of Ruthin and imprisoned him in Dolbadan Castle near Llanberis and held him to ransom. At Pilleth near Presteigne he captured Sir Edmund Mortimer — a Marcher Lord who had no particular liking for Henry IV or the English. Meanwhile Henry had his problems in France and Scotland and Edmund married Owain's daughter Jane thus assuring the allegiance for Owain of a possible future King of England: Mortimer's nephew it should be noted had a strong claim to the English throne.

In Summer 1402, central and south-east Wales were embroiled in rebellion much to the real concern of Henry who sent a huge army to Wales. In early September they invaded Wales but as they advanced, the Welsh weather came to Owain's aid and for fourteen successive days it poured. Vital stores were destroyed by water and men died of exposure. Henry's ragged army returned over the border dying on the way: The survivors were convinced that Owain was a magician who could turn the weather to his favour.

In the Spring of 1403 the English Prince of Wales, Henry (later to become Henry V) lead a powerful force into Powys and destroyed Glyndŵr's houses at Sycharth and Glyndyfrdwy.

In Summer 1403, Owain threatened Pembroke's Lordship and beseiged the English settlers within Pembroke Castle. It seemed that Owain had nearly achieved his wish. The English Parliament paid the ransom for Lord Grey of Ruthin. Mortimer (who was now Owain's brother-in-law) and Hotspur (who now no longer supported Henry IV) joined Owain and became allies. A fourth expedition of English troops failed.

The Summer of 1403 also witnessed the famous Battle of Shrewsbury between an army led by Henry IV and a rebel army led by the powerful Percy family. Hotspur (Henry Percy) was killed in one of the bloodiest battles recorded and the King won the day. It was a major blow to Owain's plans to link up with rebels and extend his hold on Wales.

However a change in fortune came when Owain allied with the French in 1404 and set up a Treaty with Charles VI of France who promised financial and material aid to Wales. Harlech and Aberystwyth fell to Owain and he was now able virtually to rule from North to South, unchallenged. Now he set up the first Welsh Parliament in Machynlleth. There were four members for each territory; educated administrators, civil servants and clerical men such as Bishop John Trevor of St Asaph. In 1405 in the presence of envoys from France and Scotland, Owain was proclaimed Prince of Wales and between Owain, the Earl of Northumberland and Sir Edmund Mortimer, they entered into a tripartite agreement whereby England and Wales would be split between them; Owain having Wales which would extend to just east of Worcester; the Earl of Northumberland having the Midlands and the northern parts of England and Sir Edmund Mortimer taking control of the south.

The French finally arrived to help Owain in 1405 when French and Welsh troops marched across Wales from the West coast in the summer of that year to reach Woodbury Hill near Worcester. Prince Henry (later Henry V) had assembled an army there and again terrible weather came to Owain's rescue. After some hesitation on Owain's part, he attacked and helped by the weather, the English retreated. Many of the French then returned home leaving some infantry men behind.

By the end of 1406, Welsh confidence was waning and English morale was growing. Many border castles and towns returned to English control. The Earl of Northumberland was in hiding and with him went any hope of Scottish aid. France had its own problems and Wales was very much alone again.

On 23 April 1406, one of Owain's sons was killed in battle leaving Maredudd as his only surviving son. Now England was less preoccupied with foreign troubles and devoted more time to strategy. Owain still held castles at Aberystwyth and Harlech and in 1407 repelled an attack by Prince Henry's troops but the next year under heavy artillary and thousands of mercenaries, Aberystwyth fell to the English and by 1409 Harlech had fallen as well. Mortimer had staunchly showed his friendship and allegiance to Owain and the Welsh by remaining to protect Aberystwyth Castle and Glyndŵr's family. He starved to death in the process. Owain's wife, two daughters and three granddaughters were all taken to London, his wife later returning to Wales.

Owain and his son Maredudd were on the run and whilst a number of Scots and French remained loyal, English power extended to nearly every part of Wales. Desperately in 1410 Owain attacked Shrewsbury and lost. His lieutenants were executed. There were no more attacks and the occupying English forces remained strong.

In 1413 Henry IV died and the former Prince Henry — now Henry V — offered Owain a pardon if he submitted to English sovereignty. Owain refused and then vanished. It was thought that he was dead by 1417 but there is no proof. Some believe Owain went to live with his daughter Alice in Herefordshire and died peacefully there. Others believe he died of cold and exhaustion on a north mountain ridge whilst some hold that he did not die at all but sleeps in some lonely mountain cave ready to come again.

There has been much criticism of Owain's 'scorched earth' policy, scouring the land of food and anything which might offer comfort or shelter to invading forces and which only heaped more material misery upon his countrymen, but Owain — this high-born Welshman — put his ambitions for a free and educated Wales beyond personal comfort. As rebellions go in those times, if length is any yard-stick, it was quite successful. The dispirited and oppressed people had some hope and purpose for over a decade and more importantly, the memory and the aims of Owain Glyndŵr have remained in the hearts and minds of the Welsh people for nearly 600 years since. If Owain did anything for his country he gave her a pride and sense of self-esteem which even six centuries have not destroyed. He struck a spark of unity which showers from each English hammer stroke seeking to manipulate or coerce this small country on the anvil of English ambition or gain.

Glyndŵr's Personal Standard & Coat of Arms
Owain Glyndŵr's personal standard was a gold dragon on a white background although according to the 'Chronicle of Adam of Usk' when he intended to attack Caernarfon on All Saint's Day in 1401 he raised a banner with a red dragon on a white background. His coat of arms are four lions rampant. For more information see ARCHAEOLOGIA CAMB. 2nd series Vol. IV 1953, pages 193-201.

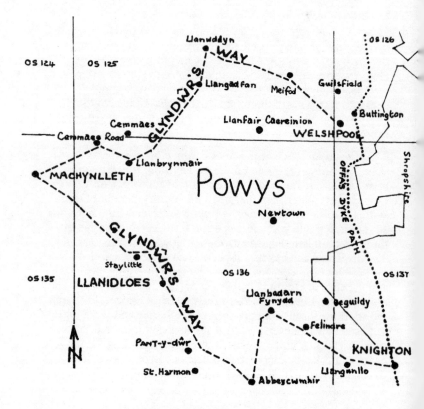

OS 124   OS 125

Llanwddyn **WAY**

Llangadfan Meifod Guilsfield

OS 126

Buttington

Cemmaes   Llanfair Caereinion   **WELSHPOOL**

Cemmaes Road GLYNDWR'S

Llanbrynmair

MACHYNLLETH   **Powys**

Shropshire

OFFA'S DYKE PATH

Newtown

GLYNDWR'S WAY

Staylittle

OS 135 **LLANIDLOES**   OS 136   OS 137

Llanbadarn Fynydd Beguildy

Felindre

Pant-y-dwr   **KNIGHTON**

St. Harmon   Llangunllo

Abbeycwmhir

N

8

GLYNDŴR'S WAY

Maps

The Maps covering the route are O.S. Landranger Series
1:50000 :-

No. 148 (Presteigne & Hay-On-Wye)
No. 136 (Newtown & Llanidloes)
No. 135 (Aberystwyth)
No. 125 (Shrewsbury)
No. 126 (Bala & Lake Vyrnwy)

Your enjoyment will be enhanced and your progress made easier
if you use the latest editions available. Forestry areas have an
annoying habit of vanishing or reproducing seemingly overnight
and their boundaries and tracks on site change constantly
making it very difficult for a cartographer to keep up-to-date.

Way-marking

Of the way-marking that does exist, the most common is the
more recent type of a standard yellow broad arrow on a square
green background. You will also come across blue arrows (which
are probably faded and weather beaten) and where you spot
them at all, know that they were the earlier types used by the
County Council.

Much of the route is on lanes and good farm tracks but there are
several sections that go onto the more remote highlands of Wales
and to which I shall refer later in the section under navigation
and safety. Do not be put off by the road walking because most
of the roads are no more than lanes which are scarcely used by
vehicular traffic and upon which you should rarely be disturbed
allowing you to enjoy high wide views — weather permitting —
whilst not always having to watch where you are putting your
feet.

As to this book itself, you will not find 'stile by stile' descriptions or maps because the route does not readily lend itself to such description. This is more in the nature of a companion to the existing route which is to be followed by use of the applicable Ordnance Survey Maps. It is a personal guide to the route known as 'Glyndŵr's Way'; a sort of unofficial companion to an unofficial long distance footpath.

The book is divided into sections of fairly short lengths which means that the walker can decide how long he or she is going to take to cover the route i.e. about 16 short days or 9 or 10 longer ones.

Accommodation will mainly be found at farmhouses and small guest houses. There are a few farms which will permit camping but who do not specifically advertise camping sites. The available listed camping sites are few and far between. Neither is the route especially well served with youth hostels apart from those in the larger towns. The prices have not been shown because they alter from time to time but at the time of publication B & B averages about £11 per person per night and evening meals between £4 and £6 each.

Navigation and Safety

Anyone who is reasonably fit and used to hill-walking can safely undertake this route but Wales is often wet and cold and at times can be very wet and very cold! Make sure you have a spare set of dry clothing particularly the luxury of dry socks for use at the end of the day's walk — and perhaps for the very last day — to see you home happy.

It cannot be stressed too much that the walker who embarks upon this route must have a sound knowledge of navigating over hill country which of course includes expertise in map reading and compass work.

As a walker who travels alone most of the time, I am never one who discourages going into the hills alone provided one is sufficiently experienced in navigation and it would always be as well that when you book ahead for your accommodation, you also inform your host of your expected time of arrival and the main points of the route which you expect to take. Do not stick doggedly to your schedule or route. If the weather changes for the worst or if the forecast is bad, take the nearest safest alternative route which from the maps you will see follow lanes or roads, although you will have a longer walk. Better to be tired from walking extra miles on lanes than carrion. You can always ring ahead to your accommodation to tell them that you will be later in those circumstances.

The best seasons for this route are late spring, early summer or early autumn. Winter would of course also be possible but frankly, on all but the crisp clear frosty days, less enjoyable.

August in Wales is notoriously wet and certainly in North Wales more rain falls during August than in any other month of the year. As will be seen from the brief history of Owain, it caused the retreat of many before us.

Animals

You may find the occasional, not to say odd, bull in a field. The law allows farmers to run non-dairy bulls aged under 11 months in a field across which a public footpath may run provided it is with cows. Frankly, no bull is to be trusted and it is best to give them as wide a berth as possible.

By far the most common animals you come across will be sheep. You will see several different breeds, the most common being the Welsh Mountain who in their pure form are all white and the lambs in particular, are extremely pretty. Other breeds will be Border Leicesters — rather superior looking white creatures with abundant wool and whose faces have an aristocratic 'Roman' profile. The pretty Beulah Speckled with their black eyes and noses and speckled faces are also quite common as are the Clun breed — distinctive with their black faces under a tuft of white fleece between black eyes with a white body and black legs. Other common breeds are the Kerry (whose home is not far from Newtown) and who are characterised by being nearly all white except for black pointed ears, black ringed eyes (giving them rather a comical appearance) and black ends of their snouts as well as black knee caps and black rear feet. You will also come across the Suffolk with their black legs, all black faces and black ears which stand akimbo.

Of non-domesticated animals and mammals, watch out for:-

Pole cats — you will be lucky to spot one of these because they emerge mostly at night from their holes and crevices. They are about 2 feet long and have a short bushy tail. They resemble a ferret but are larger.

Stoats — like the pole cat in habit but can be coloured from brown in summer to pure white in very cold winters. Both male and female have a black tip to their tail but the female is somewhat shorter than the male who is about 18 inches long.

Weasel — resemble small stoats and have short tails but they are reddy brown and have no black to their tails. The male is about a foot long, the female shorter.

Badger — you will be lucky to see a badger because again, they are nocturnal and they make their homes in woodland setts in sandy or soft soiled banks.

Otter — their homes are to be found in 'holts' in the sides of streams. They generally hunt at night although do stay out often into the morning. They are about 3½ feet long and have dark brown colouring with pale throats, small ears and a flat head.

Field Vole — greyish brown on top and greyish white underneath. About 5 inches long.

Bank Vole — these resemble small field voles but are of a more brilliant chestnut colour, slightly smaller and have a longer tail. The two types of vole (i.e. bank and field) inhabit different areas. The bank vole burrows near the surface of the ground and is about 5 inches long.

Hare — these are often seen in hilly country and live above the ground. They eat mainly field crops and feed in the evening. They have a sharp sense of hearing (one must have been quite deaf when near me near Llanbadarn Fawr as it loped towards me and was only about 2 feet away from me before it realised my presence!).

Rabbits — they are becoming more common and you will probably also see the occasional fox.

Much of the walk will take you through farmyards. This being mainly hill country, you will find that every farm has one, two or even more border collie sheep dogs. Often they are chained up but frequently they roam loose. Generally, they are quite safe but being unused to seeing walkers, if taken by surprise they will startle you by their barking and rushing at you. There is no specific guide line for advising about dealing with farm dogs. A stick is often the best method of keeping them away if you feel truly threatened. Most are only doing a job and protecting their territory and once you have left the farm, that

12

will be that. Being sheep dogs, their favourite ploy is to run behind you and have a nip at the ankle and calf of your leg. A loud 'Go!' or in Welsh 'Paid!' (don't) — pronounced 'pied' — should keep them at bay.

As to your own dog, I do not recommend that you take it at all. Even a dog on a lead will attract the inquisitive attention of young heifers and will certainly be the cause of much commotion from the other farm dogs apart from the fact that hill farmers are particularly wary of strange dogs on their land even if they appear to be under close control. As the reader will probably be aware, the law permits farmers to shoot any dog which the farmer may have cause to believe is worrying his livestock or even putting them in danger.

Birds

High Moorland/Marsh:
Curlew, whinchat, stonechats, snipe, grasshopper warblers, teal, buzzard, ravens, redshank, golden plover (particularly on Pumlumon) black grouse, red grouse, merlin (about 60 pairs in whole of Wales), ring ouzel (rare).

Farm/Field:
Long-eared owl, wren, hedge sparrow, yellow hammer, chaffinch, song thrush, goldfinch, partridge, lesser white throat, bullfinch, little owl.

Lakes/Rivers:
Dipper, common sand piper, kingfisher (quite rare), herons (plentiful), redstart, pied flycatcher (dominant species), mallard, goosanders (particularly Clywedog & Vyrnwy).

Valleys/Woodland:
Tits, tawny owls, great-spotted woodpeckers (common), green & lesser spotted woodpeckers (quite scarce), woodcock (particularly east of the Cambrian range), pied flycatchers (common), treepipit, ravens, buzzards, kite (rare but to be seen around Llanidloes and once seen never forgotten), smaller goshawk, sparrowhawk, redstarts.

Forestry:
Siskin, kite, hen harrier, short-eared owl, crossbill (scarce), firecrest (scarce).

Key Bird Watching Sites on and adjacent to Glyndŵr's Way:-

Clywedog Reservoir where will be spotted plentiful species of wild fowl including the red-breasted merganser and the passage of waders and terns in late spring and early summer.

Leighton Flats (Water meadow along the banks of the Severn south of Welshpool. Access is gained from the footpath at GR SH228042). Resident heron, mute-swan, Canada goose, mallard, meadow pipit, wagtails, great-tit, crow, raven, redpoll, reedbunting.

During December — February watch out for Bewick's swan, white-fronted goose, widgeon, gadwall pintail, snipe, curlew, redshank, peregrine, golden plover, lapwing, dipper, field-fare, redwing, siskin and brambling, goldeneye.

In March — May you may come across summer migrants passing include yellow wagtail and common sandpiper.

During June — July look out for Canada Geese in flocks and some waders.

From August to November it is the time for Swallows, passage of waders including green and wood sandpipers and green-shank.

Lake Vyrnwy (RSPB Centre at GR SH017191) Resident heron, teal, mallard, goosander, sparrowhawk, buzzard, kestrel, peregrine, falcon, red/black grouse, pheasant, moorhen, coot, black-headed gull, tawny and long-ear/short-eared owls, greater-spotted woodpecker, grey and pied wagtails, crossbill, siskin, redpoll, crow, raven, chaffinch, goldcrest, dipper.

From December to February is the time for the Whooper swan, widgeon, tufted duck, goldeneye, snowbunting.

From March to May you can see the Henharrier, merlin, golden plover, lapwing, snipe, woodcock, curlew, common sandpiper, cuckoo, blackcap, woodwarbler, chiffchaff, willow-warbler, flycatchers.

During June and July you can watch the passage of waders.

From August to November you may see common scoter, some waders and winter ducks.

From mid-October look out for field-fare and redwing.

Flowers and plants

Much grassland in the lowlands has been ploughed in the past but rough or hill grazing continue and where the Forestry Commission trees have not sprouted, you will more than likely find grazing sheep in this area of Wales. Not here will be seen the rare Snowdon lily to be found on the inaccessible crags above Cwm Idwal but nonetheless the high moorland offers an abundance of grasses and mosses. Those knee-high tussocks you struggle through will be hard mat grass (I am sure you feel better for knowing that) and which gives the uplands that pale-sheeted appearance. Lower and wetter you will find purple moor grass in which grow colonies of harebell, field woodrush and lousewort and sparkling lakes (as that is what they look like) of white cotton grass. There are about 1,400 flowering plants to be found growing wild in Wales giving rise to a wealth of plant folklore and interesting names such as Llysiau Taliesin (herbs of taliesin; brooklime) and Mary's Tears (cowslip).

Below are just a few of the more common examples which you will undoubtedly encounter along the Way:

Marsh/Moorland:
field woodrush, bell heather, lousewort, bog moss (sphagnum), marsh marigold, bog pimpernel, marsh helleborine, mountain pansy, heather, gorse, cross leaved heath, tormentil, bilberry/wimberry, broom, water crowfoot, fen orchid, mouse-ear hawkweed.

Meadow/Hedgerow:
greater stitchwort, campion, vetch, primrose, blueheath, milkwort, marsh violet, alpine strawberry, cowslip, oxlip, bluebell, harebell, ladies smock, bugle, trefoil, lesser meadow rue, water speedwell, bistort, Welsh poppy, butterbur.

Woodland/Forestry:
oak and beech ferns, wood-sorrel, enchanter's nightshade, wood anemone, ramsons, foxglove, coltsfoot.

Trees

Nearly three quarters of Wales was once covered in broad-leaved forest but, as in other parts of the World now, man destroyed the forests and this, coupled with the increased grazing of cattle and sheep over thousands of years has meant the gradual decline of natural forests. One of the main causes of woodland destruction in South Wales was the ironsmelting industry which needed charcoal and later, pitwood for the coal mines and wood for the two World Wars (when it is estimated that 60,000 acres of Welsh woodland were cleared) all took their toll. New forests were planted, notably by Forestry Commission who until very recently grew regimented rows of closely planted spruce and pine and greatly altered the face of mid and south Wales in particular. Happily, the Forestry Commission now seems also to be growing more deciduous trees and Coed Cymru, the advisory body set up to save Wales's remaining natural woodland from neglect by encouraging good management, ensure (with the help of the Countryside Commission) that about 10% of the estimated 72,000 acres of woodland at risk in Wales is now receiving some attention. Wales at last has a comprehensive and multi-purpose woodland and forestry strategy.

The most common trees you will encounter include rowan or mountain ash, sesile oak, durmast oak, alder birch, Scots pine, Douglas fir, cyprus red cedar, lodgepole pine, Norway spruce, grand fir, silver birch.

The Country Code

Guard against all risks of fire.
Keep dogs under proper control.
Keep to paths across farm land.
Leave no litter.
Safeguard water supplies.
Protect wildlife, wild plants and trees.
Go carefully on country roads.
Respect the life of the countryside.

Remember also that if you have a choice between stile and gate, always use the stile.

If you have to unfasten a gate, please re-fasten as you found it.

If you have to climb a gate, do so at the hinge-end and then one person at a time.

Getting there

Wales including, of course, the sections covered by Glyndŵr's Way, has suffered more than most areas in Britain from the erosion of public transport facilities. Do not *rely* upon public transport getting you to your overnight accommodation at the end of the day or to the start of your next day's walk. The rule of thumb is, if you see a bus, it is a bonus. However, this is not to say that none exist. In fact, in school term-time, there are certainly more frequent services in the rural areas but the drawback is that there are no reliable time-tables available for publication in a book of this sort because — through no fault of the coach operators — services seem to 'come and go' and are much more unreliable since the Government abolished the earlier regulations relating to bus services (which were with us since the 1930's) and decided to encourage competition.

There are two bus networks; the commercial network allowing operators to have services which they consider to be profitable and a network subsidised by the County Council which is supposed to compliment this and fill in any gaps. The latter services are provided by operators who have had successful tenders accepted by the County Council and companies are now free to make any changes in the services provided they give the County Council sufficient notice. Consequently, what services and time-tables there are seem to be very 'hit and miss' but do not let this discourage you from embarking upon the walk!

As far as reaching the area is concerned, the following may be helpful to you:-

Coaches

A comprehensive timetable is published by National Express twice annually: advance booking necessary via local agents.

National Express, 4 Vicarage Road Edgbaston Birmingham B15 3ES

512 London — Cheltenham — Gloucester, Hereford — one a day.
555 London — Birmingham — Shrewsbury — 5 daily of which one a day goes onto Welshpool and beyond, to Aberystwyth.

Midland Express Services Tel. (0432) 265338
Service No. X92 Birmingham — Ludlow — Hereford — 6 week days and 3 Sundays.

National Welsh Tel. (06333) 68138
Crosville (Wales) Tel. (0970) 617951
Service 700 — 'Trawscambria'. Llandudno — Wrexham —
Oswestry — Llanymynech — Welshpool — Newtown —
Llandrindod Wells — Cardiff — Barry — (Summer) on Fridays
and Saturdays.

Service No. 708 — Aberystwyth — Llanymynech — Chester —
Manchester — about 2 a week but please check for latest details.

Primrose Services — Tel. Leominster (0568) 2271

'London Flyer' — Leominster — Hereford — London. One on
Saturday only.

Rail

The rail services have actually improved over recent years.
Please check with the British Rail general time table found in
most public libraries or with British Rail direct, but the
following may be of help to you:

Crewe — Shrewsbury — Hereford —Abergavenny — Newport
— Cardiff; A regular service daily but limited on Sundays.

Shrewsbury — Knighton — Knucklas — Llanbister Road —
Llandovery — Llanelli/Swansea; (this is the 'Heart of Wales'
line which you will come across on the walk, particularly in
your early stages) — about 6 trains a day on Mondays to
Saturdays inclusive. Generally no Sunday *regular* service but a
'Rambler' service was started in 1989 on Sundays which ensured
at least 1 train a day both northbound and southbound.

Shrewsbury — Welshpool — Newtown — Machynlleth —
Aberystwyth.

For further information telephone:-

Shrewsbury (0743) 64041
Llandrindod Wells (0597) 2053
Llandovery (0550) 20398
Swansea (0792) 467777

Also, 'to help the Heart of Wales line to help you' contact:-

Heart of Wales Line Travellers Association Ref. 129,
Frankville, Broad Street, Llandovery, Dyfed SA20 0AR

18

Local Buses

Enquiry points:-

Powys County Council Llandrindod Wells (0597) 3711 Ex. 309

Primrose Motors — Tel. Leominster (0568) 2271
Owens Motors, Knighton Tel. (0547) 528303
Trefaldwyn Motors, Montgomery Tel. (068681) 277
Crosville (Wales), Oswestry Tel. (0691) 652402
National Welsh, Tel. (0970617) 951
Tanat Valley Coaches, Llanrhaeadr Tel. (069189) 241
Courtesy Cars & B-Line, Shrewsbury Tel. (0743) 58209
Llansilin Motor Services, Llansilin Tel. (069170) 318/383

Some Useful Addresses

Tourist Information centres:
The Old School, Knighton, Powys
Tel. (0547) 528753/528529

Old Town Hall, Memorial Gardens, Llandrindod Wells, Powys.
Tel. (0597) 2600

Long Bridge Street, Llanidloes
Tel. (05512) 2605

Montgomeryshire District Council Offices, Llanfyllin, Powys.
Tel. (069184) 8868

Canolfan Owain Glyndŵr, Machynlleth, Powys
Tel. (0654) 2401

Vicarage Garden Car Park, Welshpool, Powys
Tel (0938) 2043

Mid-Wales Regional Office, Wales Tourist Board, Canolfan
Owain Glyndŵr, Machynlleth, Powys.
Tel. (0654) 2653

Youth Hostel Association, South Wales Regional Office.
131 Woodville Street, Cardiff CF2 4DZ
Tel. (0222) 31370

Council for the Protection of Rural Wales. Tŷ Gwyn, 31 High
Street, Welshpool, Powys SY21 7JP (0938) 2525

Powys County Council, Planning/Leisure Services, Llandrindod
Wells, Powys LD1 5ES (0597) 3711

British Rail — see 'Getting There' section.

National Express — see 'Getting There' section.

RSPB Enquiries — Llanwddyn (069173) 278
RSPB Wales Office, Bryn Aderyn, The Bank, Newtown,
Powys. SY16 2AB Tel. (0686) 626678

Offa's Dyke Association, The Old School, West Street,
Knighton, Powys LD7 1EW. Tel. (0547) 528753

Long Distance Walker's Association, Lodgefield Cottage, High
Street, Flimwell, East Sussex. TN5 7PH.

Cardiff Weather Centre — Tel (0222) 397020

Local Information

Banks along the Way:

Barclays:
Knighton
Llanidloes
Machynlleth
Welshpool

Lloyds:
Welshpool

Midland:
Knighton
Llanfyllin
Llanidloes
Machynlleth
Meifod (possibly limited opening)
Welshpool

TSB:
Welshpool

Early Closing Days:
Knighton — Wednesday
Welshpool — Thursday
Machynlleth — Thursday
Llanidloes — Thursday

A FINAL WORD

Finally . . . a word or two for non-Welsh readers. The road and path signs and town and village names which you see on your way are written in Welsh not in order to confuse the traveller or make him or her feel unwelcome. This is the language of the country; a language well established long before the English language was in use in England, let alone in use in Wales. The sad fact that the majority of the population does not speak Welsh does not diminish its importance as the first language of the country and it is hoped that the glossary of some of the words which you will find most frequently on the maps and along your way will assist you in the walk.

Wales is not, nor ever has been, part of England. It is not a separate English region like, say East Anglia nor an English county. It is a separate country with a different culture from England and many of its people even have different values from the archetypal English person. This is not a piece of wishful thinking on my part nor a blind refusal to accept reality, nor even a voicing of an ancient and unreasonable grudge against people on the east side of the Dyke. It is a fact.

Little, proud, Wales has been threatened with extinction and exploited for many centuries and the tendancy of its people is to fight back. This is not a particularly Welsh trait but is one common to all creatures. As long as that spirit endures, the spirit of Owain Glyndŵr endures. Being of Welsh-Anglo parentage myself and whose first home was in Owain Glyndŵr's village — Glyndyfrydwy — I hope the reader will undertsand this lapse into nationalism in a walkers guide/companion but I feel it is more than relevant in a book dealing with a walk across the heartland of Wales and named after a great warrior/statesman. The spirit of Owain Glyndŵr still burns deeply in the Welsh people and I hope it will continue to do so.

All that is not to say that Wales and her people are not proud to be part of the British Isles and this is evidenced by this little country's immense contribution to Britain both in work, raw materials, culture and the blood spilt on Britain's behalf in two World Wars and in countless 'conflicts' since, but I mention the 'separateness' of this country so that the reader/walker may not only understand something more of the background to a leader like Owain Glyndŵr but also that the spirit Glyndŵr aroused is far from dead. If the traveller in Wales could respect the difference between the English and the Welsh then I am sure he or she will find a hospitality and kindness in Wales unequalled anywhere.

Croeso i Gymru — Welcome to Wales.

Clock Tower, Knighton

Glyndŵr's Way

Distances:

Knighton — Llancoch	6 miles/10km
Llancoch — Felindre	7½ miles/12 km
Felindre — Llanbadarn Fynydd	7½ miles/12 km
Llanbadarn Fynydd — Abbey-Cwmhir	7 miles/12 km
Abbey-Cwmhir — Blaentrinant	7 miles/12 km
Blaentrinant — Llanidloes	8 miles/13 km
Llanidloes — Staylittle ·	11 miles/17½ km
Staylittle — Aberhosan	6½ miles/10½ km
Aberhosan — Machynlleth	6 miles/10 km
Machynlleth — Cemmaes Road	8 miles/12 km
Cemmaes Road — Llanbrynmair	5 miles/8 km
Llanbrynmair — Llangadfan	10 miles/16 km
Llangadfan — Llanwddyn	7 miles/12 km
Llanwddyn — Dolanog	10 miles/16 km
Dolanog — Meifod	6 miles/10 km
Meifod — Welshpool	10 miles/16 km
Total:	122.5 miles/199 km

Key To Accommodation

D = Double Room
T = Twin Room
S = Single
F = Family Room
EM = Evening Meal
C = Camping Facilities
V = Vegetarians catered for
Dg = Dogs accepted

Please note:
Sketch maps are not drawn to scale. The route of Glyndŵr's
Way is shown ========= North is at the top of the page.

SECTIONS 1 & 2:   1. Knighton — Llancoch
                              2. Llancoch — Felindre

24

THE WALK

1. Knighton-Llancoch

Distance: 6 miles/10km.

Terrain: Lanes and good paths and tracks

Time: 3 hours

Map: O.S. 1:50000 Sheet 148 (Presteigne & Hay-on-Wye)

Points of Interest:

'The Narrows' in Knighton: A steep Tudor street.

Knucklas (Cnwclas). The green hill seen below you from the ridge top of Bailey Hill and the site of a Norman castle and part of which is, another castle reputed to have been lived in by Arthur and Guinevere and from which it is said that Arthur set out against the Saxons and founded the Round Table.

Camp near Fountain Head. This is situated at the top of Fron-Goch, and in 1814 some pre-Civil War coins were found. Also, near here, a strange ceremony took place for many years and until early this Century known as the Annual Election of 'The Collector of the Kings Rent' for the manor of Swydd Yr Allt. The Election of the Collector was odd in that it was held in a trench cut in the ground and the final deal was sealed when everyone concerned in the election joined hands in a hole dug at the end of the trench. The place became known as 'Holy Piece'; holy having a more secular meaning.

Llangunllo Church. 13th C. and dedicated to St. Cynllo this was rebuilt towards the end of the last Century but the tower is supposed to be one of the oldest in Wales and was then replaced by the present one. Also, this village had a monk's house and it was supposed that the monks of Abbeycwmhir came here after the Dissolution of the monasteries in 1537.

Accommodation:

Youth Hostel, West Street, *Knighton.* (0547) 528807.
1 D, 1 T, 1 S, EM&V (by arrangement), Dg.

Mrs A. Bodenham, Gwernaffel Farm, *Knighton,* LD7 1SE. (0547) 528650.
1 D, 1 T, 1 S, EM&V (by arrangement), Dg.

Mrs. A.B. Johnson, Rose Offa, George Road, Cwm, *Knighton.* LD7 1HL. (0547) 528563.

1 T (en suite), Tea/Coffee making facilities, (TV), V.

Mrs. O. Mival, (Off route), 3, Penybont Road, Whitton, Nr *Knighton*. (05476) 241.
1 T, EM (by arrangement), C, V.

1. The route starts from the Clock Tower in Knighton — which bears a similar resemblance to another Clock Tower we shall meet later in the journey — about mid-way at Machynlleth. Go along the steep street known as 'The Narrows' and enter the Llandrindod Road.

2. Turn right at Brook House Farm, opposite entrance to the Teme Valley Fox Hound Kennels.

3. Follow the course of Wylcwm Brook, passing Lower & Little Cwmgilla and Ebrandy house where turn left and follow the straight forward track west, climbing Bailey Hill.

4. After two and half kilometres from Ebrandy and having topped Bailey Hill, you enter a lane that runs along the ridge and from here you should see Knucklas below.

5. Turn left onto the lane, and still walking upwards, follow the lane past Upper Dolwalkin to Fountain Head enjoying the ridge panoramic views. This area is typical of the high wide hills of the borders; remote yet strangely benign.

6. At Fountain Head, a lane leads westward from Glyndŵr's Way towards Llangunllo, (one and a half miles). You will probably notice that Fountain Head is surrounded by springs. As Fountain Head comes into sight, take the track leading off right — still continuing a westerly direction (To the left of this lane is the large camp which is actually off your route).

7. Continuing along the track westerly, (see if you can see the enormous buzzard family hereabouts!) your route will pass above Frongoch and gently descend then level slightly as you head north. You will be in a green lane which drops west again to Llancoch, a very small hamlet near the Heart of Wales Railway line.

8. Turn left at the minor road and follow across the entrance of the Railway tunnel to a grass triangle. Here you should see a way-mark to point you towards Ferley, still travelling westward.

2. Llancoch-Felindre

Distance: 7½ miles/12km

Terrain: Some tracks but mostly open moorland

Time: 4 hours

Maps: O.S. 1:50000. Sheet 136 (Newtown and Llanidloes)

Points of Interest:

Short Ditch. Constructed by Sir Edmund Mortimer around 1400 as a defence against Owain Glyndŵr's forces who threatened Knighton.

Beacon Hill. The round barrows found around the top of the Beacon Hill date from the Bronze Age and the hill itself was probably used for beacon fires to give warning of danger or pass news of importance.

Felindre. A small village with only an inn and a few houses.

Accommodation:

Mrs. Jean Reynolds, Rhydycwm, *Felindre*, Nr. Knighton.
LD7 1YS. (05477) 232.
1 F, 1 D, EM, C, V, Dg.

1. From the minor road at Llancoch follow the way marks westward towards Ferley (from the Welsh — 'fferllyd' — meaning 'open to the elements'). Your way is well defined along a track. Continue beyond Ferley, heading northwards over the heather-covered rampart known as Short Ditch.

2. After Short Ditch, enter open hill and head north-west with Pool Hill on your left and source of the River Lugg below (and out of sight!) and with Beacon Hill with its tumuli on your right. There is no way-marking but you should enjoy the views although in poor visibility, compass bearings will be necessary. It is possible to follow a well-defined track around Pool Hill although you will be on open moorland.

3. South of Beacon Hill, take a bridleway west and continue over the slopes of Stanky Hill.

4. At GR 172765 go northwards skirting Black Mountain on your right and continue north-east to Cefn Pawl. From here, you will have beautiful views over the Teme Valley and to the Kerry Hills beyond.

6. Beyond Cefn Pawl, take the path continuing north around the hill and reach the edge of Millwood.

7. Continue around the edge of the wood and then east to Brandy House Farm.

8. Take farm lane to reach road where turn left to enter Felindre.

Near Tumuli (west of Felindre)

3. Felindre-Llanbadarn Fynydd

Distance: 7½ miles/12 km

Terrain: Good tracks and some lanes

Time: 4 hours

Map: O.S. 1:50000 Sheet 136 (Newtown & Llanidloes)

Points of Interest:

Mounds near Crug y Byddar. Two elevated mounds on opposite banks of the River Teme which were once connected by a ridge of earth of about half a mile in length. The larger (north-east) is thought to have been the home of Utyr Pendragon, the father of King Arthur. 'Pendragon' means dragon's head or 'Chief of dragons'. (Owain Glyndŵr later adopted a two-legged dragon as his standard).

Tumuli near Fiddlers Green Farm. 3 Bronze Age tumuli in the form of round barrows on northern end of Rhiw Porthnant.

Llanbadarn Fynydd. In English meaning 'the Church of St. Padarn amid hills'. Padarn was a 6th C. Saint and a follower of St. David, the Patron Saint of Wales.

Badarn Fynydd. Supposedly was surrounded by 20 — 30 earth forts and it is possible that the place Badarn is where Arthur fought his last battle. The Church is another example of a 13th C. Church being rebuilt in the last century. It has a 15th C. screen and the alter rails date to 1716.

Accommodation:

J. R. and G.J. Hayman, New Inn, *Llanbadarn Fynydd*, LD7 6YA. (059783) 224.
2 D, EM, C, V, Dg.

Mrs. E.A. Powell, 'Woodlands', *Llanbadarn Fynydd*, LD7 6YA. (059783) 328.
D, S and F available, C, V, Dg. (but not in house).

Mrs. E. Nicholls, (Off route), Bwlch Farm, *Llananno*, LD1 6TT. (059783) 232.
1 D, 1 S, 1 F, EM, V.

1. From Felindre turn left after the Inn and then right at Upper House Farm entering a green way which goes west and up on to a spur towards Rhosgoch. On your way you will see the Teme Valley and a short way to the north is Crug-y-Byddar and the two mounds you should see on opposite banks of the Teme.

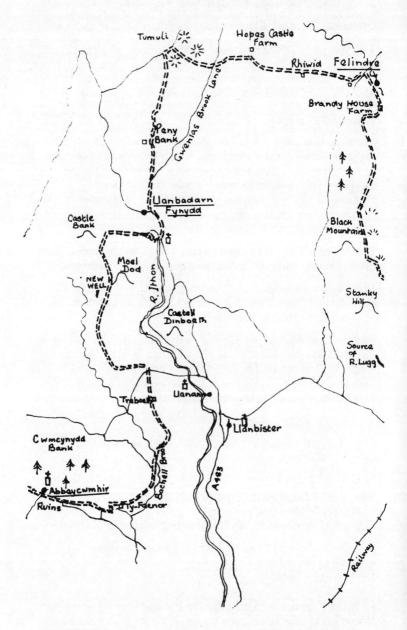

SECTIONS 3 & 4:   3. Felindre — Llanbadarn Fynydd
                                   4. Llanbadarn Fynydd — Abbey Cwmhir

30

2. Continue westward along track which rises slightly up Rhuvid Bank to reach Hopes Castle Farm. Here enjoy the extensive views as you walk down (west) and across Gwenlas Brook.

3. After the brook, take the path left that goes to the west of Fiddlers Green Farm where you will see the Bronze Age tumuli.

4. From the tumuli, turn left onto lane and take the first turning off to the left (heading now south south-west) and follow the road for about two and a half miles descending to Llanbadarn Fynydd village, delightfully situated by the River Ithon.

4. Llanbadarn Fynydd — Abbey-Cwmhir

Distance: 7½ miles/12 km

Terrain: Good lanes and farm tracks and some hill paths

Time: 4 hours

Maps: O.S. 1:50000. Sheet No. 136 (Newtown & Llanidloes)

Points of Interest:

Castelltinboeth. Although the route does not pass this site, the site of Castelltinboeth is unmistakeable from Tŷn-y-pant Farm as you look east across the valley. This is a fortification on a 1,400 ft high hill and the name is thought to derive from Maud de Breos who died in 1301 and was the wife of Roger Mortimer, one of the Marcher Lords. Also, it may earlier have been the home of Cadwallon Madoc who is the probable founder of Abbey-Cwmhir and who was killed by Mortimers in 1179. The fortification is bounded by a deep moat and fragments of a tower remain. Historians say that the castle was finally demolished by Llewellyn Gruffudd in 1260. The remains of a pre-historic hill fort can also be seen on the hill.

Ty Faenor. A Manor House built from the ruins of Abbey-Cwmhir during the reign of James I. In 1696 nine windows were bricked up and converted to cupboards as a result of the window tax. The house contains some beautiful 17th C. woodwork including a solid oak doorway and original attic door as well as an early 14 C. staircase which is older than the house itself.

Abbey-Cwmhir. A Cistercian Abbey founded in 1143 by Cadwallon Madoc who ruled the whole country from the River Severn to the Wye and who was descended from the founder of the fifth Royal Tribe of Wales. The building was not completed, although it was planned to be one of the largest in Britain. In 1401 Owain Glyndŵr destroyed the Abbey after he discovered that most of the monks were English spies of Henry V. The Dissolution of the monasteries by Henry VIII in 1536 successfully put an end to the Abbey's existence.

Accommodation:

Mrs. N.K. Morris, Mill Cottage, *Abbey Cwmhir*, LD1 6PH.
No tel. but can be contacted on (059787) 666.
1 D, 1 S, 1 T, EM, V.

Mrs. G. A. Hamer, Home Farm, *Abbey Cwmhir*, LD1 6PH.
(059787) 666.
1 D, 1 F, EM, C, V, Dg.

1. At Llanbadarn Fynydd, take the bridge over the River Ithon and continue along the lane around a sharp left hand bend to some cross roads.

2. At cross roads turn right (west) and follow a stony track (Be careful not to go too far right and back down the hill!)

3. Follow the stony track until it peters out on the slopes of Garn Hill. Care will be needed after the end of the track and reliance will have to be placed upon map and compass. However, if you go to the head of the valley which is to the south of a saddle between Castle Bank and Moel Dod, you then turn south and soon leave the valley and skirt the northern edge of Yr Allt, climbing slightly and veering east. (Shortly you should see ruins of Castelltinboeth on your left).

4. Pass through Tŷn-y-pant Farm and reach the road. (If you encounter a gander — I am told it is quite safe but err on the side of caution and give it a wide berth).

5. At the road, you should see a sign-post pointing south to Bwlch Farm. Take this and at Bwlch go south but not along the lane to Treboeth. Instead climb towards the summit above known as Ysgwd-ffordd.

6. At the saddle of the hill and south of the hill, head south-west descending steeply through Neuadd-Fach Woods and over Bachell Brook and back onto the road.

7. On lane turn left and head south through this beautiful section keeping the brook on your left until you reach Ty-faenor. Just past Ty-faenor is a gate and immediately after that, the route goes right through another gate to enter another lane. Keep to the valley and head west for about 3 miles to reach Abbey Cwmhir (Alternatively at Ty-faenor, keep to the lane and at T junction, turn right and follow for a mile to Abbey-Cwmhir.)

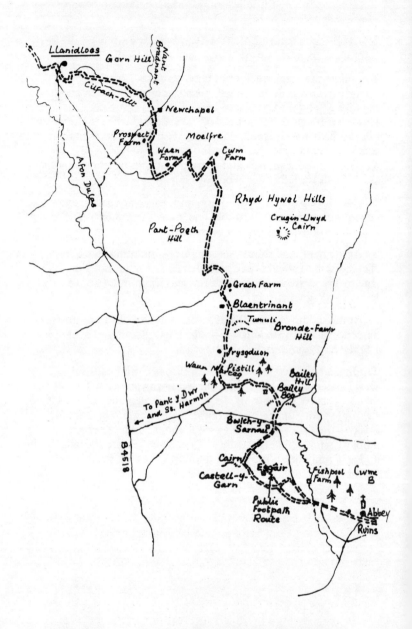

SECTIONS 5 & 6:   5. Abbey Cwmhir — Blaentrinant
6. Blaentrinant — Llanidloes

34

5. Abbey-Cwmhir — Blaentrinant

Distance: 7 miles/12 km

Terrain: Mainly forest tracks and some lanes

Time: 3 hours

Map: O.S. 1:50000. Sheet 136 (Newtown & Llanidloes)

Points of Interest:

Abbey Cwmhir Church. Victorian but in the Gothic style and dedicated to St Mary the Virgin.

The Happy Union Inn. Has a sign depicting a man with a leek in his hat, astride a goat and holding an ale jug aloft. The sign has been in existence for many years but its origins are unknown.

'The Monk's Way'. Part of the early stage of the walk from the Abbey through the forest from the Inn joins with this ancient track which may have been used as a route by the monks of Abbey-Cwmhir and Strata Florida, Dyfed.

Castell-y-garn. A burial chamber in which was found a stone chest full of human bones on the summit of the highest hill on this section of the walk, Castell–y-garn is believed to date from the Bronze Age.

Domen Ddu. This literally means 'a black burial mound' and is near the small holding, Prysgduon.

Grave of Llewellyn. This last true Prince of Wales: The actual site of his grave is unknown. He was killed at Cilmeri near Builth Wells in December 1282, his head taken to London and put on show and, according to tales, his remains buried in a field near Abbey Cwmhir.

Accommodation:

Difficult! Nearest may be at Pant-y-dwr and St. Harmon — this is not on the route but about 4½ miles away from Bwlch-y-sarnau and about 6 miles from Abbey-Cwmhir by road. Check latest situation by contacting Tourist Information office at Rhayader. (0597) 810591.

1. Opposite the Happy Union Inn, take the track through the forest (the Monk's Way) and head north-west through woodland. After about three-quarters of a mile, cross a minor

road by going left then right. The path goes behind some houses before taking a forest track again in the same north-westerly direction. An alternative is to turn right on entering the lane and walk to Fishpool Farm then turn left along the track and continue into the forest. (N.B. The public footpath does not enter the forest but heads up the shallow spur (north-westerly) over Upper Esgair Hill).

2. Continue along the forest track for about one and a half miles heading north-westerly all the time and when you leave the forestry, you will be very near the summit of Castell-y-garn.

3. From Castell-y-garn, head north-west and descend slightly for about half a mile to join the lane at Blwch-y-sarnau. This is a high moorland hamlet and you will probably now be feeling the first 'wildness' of the walk. If the weather is good, you should have your first views of Pumlumon and Cadair Idris.

4. From the lane at Bwlch-y-sarnau, you continue by the road to Llaithddu (heading north-east) to the point where it is signposted at a track which heads off the ridge to the north and named 'Bailey Bog'. Continue on this track to Brondrefach.

5. From Brondrefach turn west (left) along a forestry track through woodland for about three-quarters of a mile.

6. At a T junction in forestry, turn left and proceed for about a third of a mile until you reach a lane where turn right (heading north-west again) and follow the lane for about a mile after which you should see the route sign pointing right (north-east).

7. At this junction, take the north easterly course following a track to Prysgduon about half a mile distant.

8. From Prysgduon, continue along the track, keeping to the left hand edge of the forestry for some of the way until you leave the forestry but continue north to Blaentrinant, contouring the edge of the hillside.

6. Blaentrinant — Llanidloes

Distance: 8miles/13km

Terrain: Mainly forest tracks and lanes — roughish section between Graig and Waen Farm

Time: 4 hours

Map: O.S. 1:50000. Sheet 136 (Newtown & Llanidloes)

Points of Interest:

Cairns at Pegwm Bach and Pegwm Mawr Two Bronze Age Cairns, one on each top and about ¼ mile to the east of the Way.

Newchapel. Can be viewed from the road near Prospect Farm. Built in 1740 by Baptist and Independent Non-Conformists but with the decline of the Non-Conformists it became a Baptist only chapel.

Llanidloes. The first town on the banks of the River Severn being 10 miles from this source. The first Christian settlement was made here in the early 7th C. by St. Idloes.

Llanidloes Church. Note magnificent arches, said to have come from Abbey-Cwmhir after the Dissolution in 1536 and also the south doorway. There is a 14 C. clock mechanism but no clock face in the Church tower: the font and some of the windows are said to date from the early 15th C. Note also the hammer-beam roof.

The Catholic Church. Named after St. Richard Gwyn (Martyr). Richard Gwyn was a Roman Catholic who disagreed with the Reformation and was burnt at the stake in Wrexham in 1584.

The Old Market Hall. A magnificent timber-framed building and the oldest surviving example of its type in Wales and in its time having been a Quaker Meeting House, both a Weslyan and Baptist converticle, a Public Library, a Working Men's Institute and a Wool Market as well as a Court House. The Market is held every Saturday and is a result of a Grant to the Prince of Powys by Edward I.

The Mount Inn Stands on the site of Llanidloes Castle (of which there are no visible remains).

Accommodation:

John & Shirley Knight, Dwy Afon, Frankwell, *Llanidloes*, SY18
6HE. (055122) 3573.
1 T, 2 D, EM. V. Dg. — (not in house)

Mrs. B. C. Lines, Gorphwysfa, Westgate Street, *Llanidloes*,
SY18 6HL. (05512) 3356.
2 D, 1 T, 1 S, 1 F, EM, V, Dg.

B. Wildgoose, The Mount Inn, China Street, *Llanidloes*.
(05512) 2247.
1 D, 1 T, (En suite, tea/coffee making facilities), EM, V.

B. and C. M. Jones, Royal Head, Shortbridge Street, *Llanidloes*.
(05512) 2583.
All types of room available, EM, V.

1. From Blaentrinant pass an old quarry and cross a stream by
Grach Farm, the route having wound its way north to the farm.

2. From the farm, continue north to a stream, and follow for a
while and then cross to Grid ref. 007805.

3. Head east (right) to the wood edge at GR 011814 and
continue along the edge and then north as the way bends back
left to Grid Ref. 011817.

4. A track then goes left and down hill towards Cwm Farm. Do
not go into the farm but take the path as it turns left to follow
and cross the stream.

5. Follow the stream for only a few hundred yards before
turning right (north) to go around the edge of a small hill to
reach Waen Farm. (This is a route-finding headache!)

6. From the Farm head south-west to join the lane.

7. At lane, turn right for less than ¼ mile and take the next
track on the right which is a green lane and pass between rows
of hazel trees heading north to the road.

8. At road, go right and into Newchapel.

9. At the Chapel in Newchapel, turn left (north-west) for about
¼ mile and left again, leaving the road to descend to cross the
Nant Bradnant in wooded valley.

10. Ascend from Nant Bradnant slightly heading west until you
reach a lane and follow this into Llanidloes with Lletty Coch-
nant beside you. (The colour of the stream is not due to blood-it
is called 'The Red Brook' due to its mineral content, haematite).

7. Llanidloes — Staylittle

Distance: 11 miles/17½km

Terrain: Woodland, some fields & forestry tracks and lanes

Time: 6 hours

Map: O.S. 1:50000. Sheet 136 (Newtown and Llanidloes)

Points of Interest:

Long Bridge. This part of the River Severn once had a bridge that was believed to be haunted by Lady Jeffreys who was infamous in her day towards the end of the 19th C. Sometimes a water spirit, she then used to lodge just below Short Bridge in order to watch the ivy grow. This came from the arches and if the ivy joined near the key-stone on the bridge, she could rest in peace. As the ivy was continually cut, her ghost would often appear until the old bridge was blown up in 1848.

Frankwell. The name of this area derives from the Middle Ages when Flemish Weavers settled in this area. As they were not allowed to live in the towns, they stayed outside the town walls.

Market Hall, Llanidloes

Fan Mine. Much lead was mined here in 1865 creating a bonanza in the area and at its peak employing over 700 men. The lead and zinc ore was carried by standard gauge railway specially built for this purpose and linking with the Cambrian Railway at Caersws, 6 miles away.

Bryntail. A lead and barytes mine near Clywedog Dam.

Clywedog Dam. 212ft high and holding back 6½ miles length of the Llyn Clywedog completed in 1967 and controlling the flow of the River Severn to prevent flooding in times of high rain-fall. Holds 11,000 million gallons of water. Popular for water sport. Wild life in the area includes grey squirrels, common pole cats, foxes and short tailed vole.

Pen-y-Gaer. Site of an Iron Age fort.

Hafren Forest. Hafren is the Welsh name for Severn, the source of which lies in the Pumlumon hills about 4 miles west. A huge forest of 18 sq. miles of plantation managed by the Forestry Commission is the home for much in the way of wild life and fungus. A leaflet is available from the Forestry Commission Offices.

Staylittle. 'Penfforddlas' in Welsh and literally meaning 'the end of the green road' — so named because the local blacksmith was so expert and shod travellers' horses so quickly that they needed to 'stayalittle'. It was a popular stop-over place for the drovers and their large herds as they made their treks into England in the 18th & 19th C.

The Quaker Cemetery above the Village. The immediate vicinity had a large Quaker (now also known as Religious Society of Friends) population in late 17th & early 18th C.

Accommodation:

Nearest at *Dylife*. (See next section.)

1. Leave Llanidloes along Long Bridge Street, crossing Long Bridge and then turn left along the B4518.

2. Take the second turning on the right, the road to Van (Fan) and follow this for 1½ miles into the old village itself beside the old lead mines, an especially interesting part for industrial archeologists.

3. From the village, turn west along a lane to the house at the end. From here head slightly south and then up the hill to Pen-y-Clun. (This is the way of the County Council route but there

is some doubt as to whether it is a definite right of way. The actual right of way goes along the valley of the stream, crosses the stream and contours around the hillock to Pen-y-Clun.) Thence go up the farm lane to the road, cross the road and take the path down to the Old Mines of Bryn-y-tail.

4. From Bryn-y-tail, you will emerge directly beneath Clywedog Dam. The route continues along the minor road towards the southern end of the reservoir. On your left is Pen-y-Gaer, an Iron Age hill fort.

5. After Pen-y-Gaer, at a white house, turn right, making sure you head north-west towards the water's edge of Clywedog Reservoir.

6. At the edge of the Reservoir, follow edge of water to the road. Then turn right and follow this road for many miles winding along the banks of the reservoir through forestry and for the most part heading north, until you reach Staylittle. On your way, you will cross Afon Biga and after passing through forestry, about 1 mile later you will cross over Afon Llwyd. 3 miles to the west of this latter point is the valley of Afon Hyddgen where in 1401 Owain Glyndŵr beat stronger forces in a battle and his success in this ensured that anyone who had previously wavered about his cause did so no longer and followed him.

Clywedog Reservoir

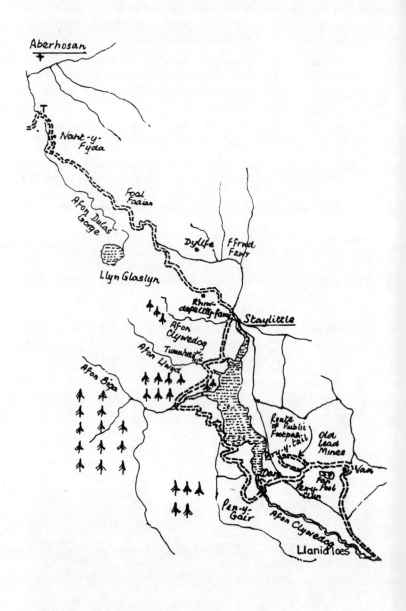

SECTIONS 7 & 8:   7. Llanidloes — Staylittle
                      8. Staylittle — Aberhosan

8. Staylittle — Aberhosan

Distance: 6½ miles/10½km

Terrain: Ancient trackways over wild moorland and short road section

Time: 3½ hours

Map: O.S. 1:50000. Sheet 136 (Newtown and Llanidloes)

Points of Interest:

Penycrocbren Hill The track which goes over this is an ancient Roman road later used as a drovers and coach road from Llanidloes to Machynlleth. Look for the ruts of the old wheels beneath your feet! On the summit of the hill itself just before the path descends is the site of the Roman fort. It is almost certain that the Dylife mines were worked for lead by the Romans. This was also known as Gallows Hill in the 18th C. when this mode of execution was popular.

Dylife (literally 'place of the flood') The Way does not go through Dylife but passes near to this old hamlet which in the middle of the last century exceeded 1,000 people mainly earning their living from the lead and copper mines.

Aberhosan ('mouth of the River Rhosan'). This village was famous for its craftsmen who made the famous bardic chairs for the Eisteddfodau. (The Way does not pass through the village but to the south of it).

Accommodation:

Dylife — (Off main route) Tony and Sue Banks, The Star Inn, Dylife, Nr. *Staylittle*, Llanbrynmair. SY19 7BW. (06503) 345. All types of room available, EM, C, V, Dg. (By arrangement).

1. From the Quaker cemetery at Staylittle, turn left along lane and pass Rhiw-defeitty-fawr Farm and on reaching an open hillside head uphill and west towards the top of Penycrocben (For more beautiful views and accommodation — leave the route here and continue north to Ffrwd Fawr a lovely water-fall at the head of Afon Twymyn; then left (west) along lane into Dylife. From Dylife continue west along lane to rejoin the Way at Bryn y Fedwen (GR 836952)).

2. Beyond Pen-y-Crocbren, the path descends, passing through some woodland and alongside the bank of a pond and along a farm entrance before reaching the mountain road.

3. On entering the mountain lane, turn left and head north-east to GR836952 where turn left. Follow a track for a while and head north-west towards the trig point of Foel Fadian. On a clear day, ahead you should see Glaslyn ('the blue lake') and beyond that, Pumlumon. In this high upland, Owain Glyndŵr raised his standard and the stone cairn at the eastern end of Nant-y-Moch Dam commemorates that. The Way passes slightly to the south of Foel Fadian but you may feel like a diversion to take this in.

4. From this point, follow Nant-Fadian a short way north-west to Nant-y-Fyda. (Leave the Way here by heading steeply up lane (north) then down to Aberhosan if you plan to stay in the village. Next day, re-trace your steps to Nant-y-Fyda).

Above Foel Fadian

9. Aberhosan — Machynlleth

Distance: 6 miles/10 km

Terrain: Roads and tracks, some steep

Time: 3 hours

Map: O.S. 1:50000. Sheet 135 (Aberystwyth)

Points of Interest:

Ogo Wyddan Roman copper mines near Machynlleth Town Golf Course.

Machynlleth Charter granted to the town in 1291 by Edward I. Fine architecture in particular the black and white timbered section of the Owain Glyndŵr Institute (18th C.) which is now the office of the Mid-Wales Tourist Council and a cafe but used to be the town baths. The oldest part of the building is 16th C. and is supposed to be the same site where Glyndŵr held his first Parliament in 1402 and now holds the town Library and Museum. Royal House used to be the town jail where King Charles I was held prisoner. He is reputed to have escaped via an underground passage to the river. The river bridge over the Dyfi was first built in 1533 and rebuilt about 1800. The Romans had a camp/fort at Pennal on the opposite side of the Dyfi and had look-out points on the Wylfa and Fron y Gog, two of the hills overlooking the town. The present church is on the site of an early medieval church. The Corris Railway is one of the many narrow gauge Welsh railways and was originally built for the slate quarries to take slate through Machynlleth to Derwen Quay on the Estuary.

Accommodation:

David and Diana Timms, Rhiwlwyfen, *Forge*, Nr. Machynlleth. SY20 8RP. (0654) 2683.
All types of room. EM, (By arrangement), C (limited), V.

1. From Nant-y-Fyda, enter the lane going north-west and continue on this, following Afon Dulas.

2. Beyond the telephone box, take the lane south (left) and at the first farm, turn right (west) and start climbing Cefn Modfedd, a tiny hill. Do not follow track south-west, but head north-west and descend the hill by another track to Blaen-y-Pant.

3. At the minor road, turn right and at the first fork, turn left.

4. This turns sharply to the left shortly and later reaches a cattle grid. Here, turn left and then bear right (north) at Henllan Farm. Pass between some copses and enter a delightful green lane and follow this to the village of Forge.

5. From Forge, follow the road, crossing the Golf Course and enter Machynlleth by the main street, Heol Maengwyn.

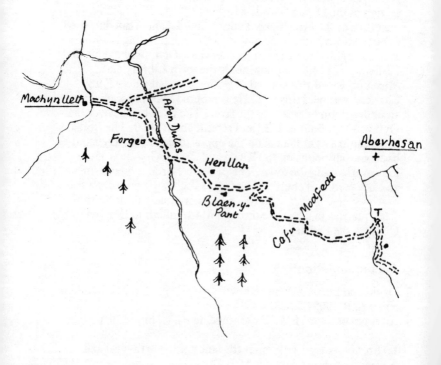

SECTION 9:   Aberhosan — Machynlleth

10. Machynlleth — Cemmaes Road

Distance: 8 miles/12km

Terrain: Road and tracks, some open hill tops and woods including some stiffish climbs

Time: 4 hours

Map: O.S. 1:50000. Sheet 135 (Aberystwyth)

Points of Interest:

Penegoes. A small village founded in the middle of the 6th C. by the Celtic Saint Cadfarch. In 1198, much of the land in the Parish was granted to the monks of the Cistercian Monastery of Strata Marcella. In English Penegoes literally means 'head of Egoes'. He was a legendary Celtic chief and his head was said to be buried beneath some oak trees beyond the church. There is a group of cottages called Craig yr Henfordd (stone of the old street). The road here is probably of Roman foundation and there remains a Roman well in the village. The village was also the birth place of the 18th C. landscape artist Richard Wilson whose paintings can be seen in the National Portrait Gallery in London and in the Manchester Art Gallery.

Abercegir. Once famous for its woollen mills but not productive for many years.

Mathafarn. An historic house about a mile west of Cemmaes Road on the north of the Dyfi. Owain Glyndŵr is reputed to have stayed here and there is supposedly a secret underground path running from a house to his Parliament House in Machynlleth.

Accommodation:

Mr. & Mrs. David & Diana Timms (See also last section). Rhiwlwyfen, *Forge,* Machynlleth. SY20 8RP (0654) 2683 D, T, S and F available, EM (If advance booked), Limited Camp, V.

Mrs. E. O. Harris, Cefn Coch Uchaf, *Cemmaes Road,* Machynlleth. (065 02) 552 1 D, 1 S. (F room can be arranged) EM, Camp, V, Dg.

Olivia Chandler (See also next section). 'Gwalia', *Commins Coch,* Machynlleth SY20 9PU (06502) 377 (GR 853048) (50yds from 'Way') 1 T, 1 F, Veg *only,* EM, Camp, Dg.

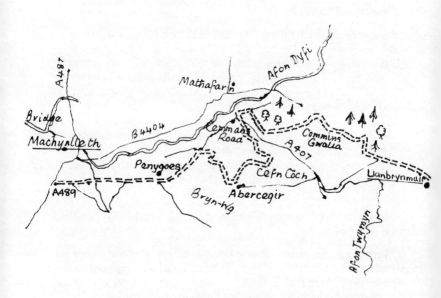

SECTIONS 10 & 11:   10. Machynlleth — Cemmaes Road
                        11. Cemmaes Road — Llanbrynmair

Pendre, Maengwyn Street, *Machynlleth*. SY20 8EF. (0654) 2088. 2 D/T, 1 F, EM.

The White Lion Hotel, Heol Pentreheydw, Machynlleth. SY20 8ND. (0654) 3455.
All types of room available, EM.

Maenllwyd, Newtown Road, *Machynlleth*. SY20 8EY. (0654) 2928. 5 D/T, 2 F, EM.V. Dg.

1. From Machynlleth head east along the A489, cross Afron Dulas and continue to the village of Penegoes.

2. Continue on main road for about a mile and then turn right up a track (south-east). It is to be hoped you have the clear views of Cadair Idris and the Dyfi Valley from here.

3. The route continues skirting Bryn-wg and enters the village of Abercegir, passing on your way a ruined woollen mill.

4. From the main street of the village, turn left and sharply right at a junction and continue for less than a quarter of a mile along the lane and then turn left, taking the lane which leads off and up the hill. The track is not very well defined but becomes more so as you reach the ruin of Gader-goch.

5. You find yourself on the summit ridge of Cefn Coch and continue in a north-easterly direction to reach a green lane. Continue along this until you meet a cross-road of lanes. (You should encounter most beautiful views north).

6. At the cross-roads of the lanes, turn left and follow that lane for 1 mile to the main road (heading north-west).

7. At the main road, turn left and follow this for ¼ mile to the roundabout.

8. Take the A470 Dolgellau road (north-east). (Mathafarn is across the Dyfi about a mile away to the west.)

Parliament House, Machynlleth

49

11. Cemmaes Road — Llanbrynmair

Distance: 5 miles/8km

Terrain: Good pathways, lanes and tracks.

Time: 2½ hours

Map: Series 1:50000 — Sheet 136 (Newtown & Llanidloes)

Points of Interest:

Cemmaes Church. Founded in the 6th C. by Saint Tydacho who came to Wales from Britanny and had magical powers attributed to him. He is a source of many Welsh legends.

Llanbrynmair. (Hill Church of Mary). A small town but reputed to have the highest emigration rate in Wales. (If you reach here tired and wet, you will probably understand why).

Llanbrynmair Parish Church. This is outside the village, two miles along the Staylittle Road, in the village of Llan. Dates from the 7th and 12th C. Very old belfry made out of four large pillars of oak.

Stone Circles on Newydd Fynyddog. Situated near Llanbrynmair and the Upper Rhedd Valley and only 450ft apart. One is known as Cerrig Gaerall and is 69ft in diameter. The other circle has a maximum diameter of 85ft, four stones surviving in this one with 3 being in situ.

Accommodation:

Olivia Chandler, *Commins Coch*. (*50yds. off 'Way'*). (For details see last section).

1. From Cemmaes Road take the main A470 road towards Dolgellau crossing the bridge over the River Twymyn.

2. Over bridge, turn right along the track up the Twymyn Valley along the railway and gradually ascend a small valley and enter open hillside.

3. After about half mile, your path joins a track which takes you down to a lane at Commins Gwalia. On lane turn right and follow for ¼ mile until the lane swings right.

4. From here, turn left along a track. You are at 1,290 ft and should have lovely views of the Dyfi Valley and Afon Twymyn.

5. After ⅔ mile, the track leads onto another minor road. Turn right onto minor road – which crosses open moorland near Waen Fawr – and descend valley to reach the main A470 road again.

6. Turn left at main road and after about a mile and a half you reach the village of Llanbrynmair.

Owain Glyndŵr Centre, Machynlleth

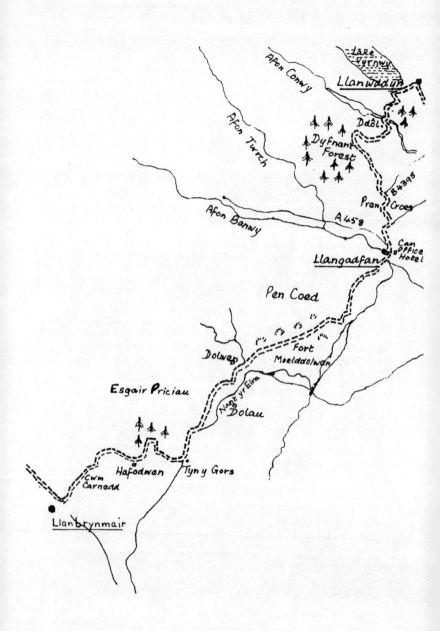

SECTIONS 12 & 13: 12. Llanbrynmair — Llangadfan
13. Llangadfan — Llanwddyn

12. Llanbrynmair — Llangadfan

Distance: 10 miles/16km

Terrain: Moorland (little shelter and no refreshment available — one of the longest sections of this walk between points of 'civilisation').

Time: 4 hours

Maps: Series 1:50000 Sheet: 136 (Newtown & Llanidloes) & Sheet: 125 (Bala & Lake Vyrnwy)

Points of Interest:

Cwm Carnedd. (Valley of stones). This tumili allegedly marks the grave of an infamous robber called Owain. On one of his sorties, he was chased, his stirrups broke and he was captured, killed and buried on this small hill.

Moel Ddolwen Fort. Atop Ddolwen Hill, oblong surrounded by ditches and earth walls with extensive views towards Llanerfyl and Llanfair.

Llangadfan. Named after St.Cadfan, one of the many 6th C. saints who came to Wales from Britanny and is considered the Patron Saint of Warriors.

The Cann Office Hotel. Built on the site of an old fortress and the earth works remain near the hotel comprising mound and Bailey Castle of the Norman type. The hotel itself was a famous posting house in Wales during the coaching era.

Accommodation:

Cann Office Hotel, *Llangadfan*, Powys. (093888) 202.
All types of room available, Enquire direct as to EM, V, C or Dg.

1. The route of Glyndŵr's Way from Llanbrynmair has been the subject of some controversy in the last 10 years. It is hoped that you will now find it adequately way-marked in the area of controversy — namely Cwm Carnedd — but if you do not do so, I recommend leaving Llanbrynmair along the A470 and taking the lane left by a telephone kiosk. Cross the railway.

2. Continue along the lane beside the Old Chapel on the other side of the railway and follow to Cwm Carnedd Isaf.

3. From here, take the lane north-east (right) to Hafodwen. Now you will need good map reading.

4. The track is often indistinct but head east towards the forestry plantation. Do not attempt to go through it — it is impenetrable. Pass to the north of the plantation and follow a fence going east. (You will be trespassing but the right of way through forest *is* difficult.)

5. Along this fence set your compass and head south-east over moorland through the ruins of Tyn-y-Gors.

6. From the ruin, follow a green lane to the road.

7. At the road, turn left (north) and follow this heading generally northwards crossing River Garn and following its valley. After about 2½ miles, you will pass a chapel on your left. Shortly afterwards, the road crosses Afon Cannon and in about ¾ of a mile, take a lane on your left towards Dolwen Farm.

8. Bear right heading first north-east then quickly east then north-east again taking the route below the fort on Moelddolwen. You now enter open moorland which you stay with for at least 2 miles.

9. Descend to a lane and continue on the lane to reach a minor road, on your way crossing a ford. At the road, turn left and descend northerly into Llangadfan.

Bridge over Afon Gam (south of Llangadfan)

13. Llangadfan — Llanwddyn

Distance: 7 miles/12km

Terrain: : Roads and good forestry tracks

Time: 3½ hours

Map: O.S. 1:50000. Sheet 125 (Bala & Lake Vyrnwy)

Points of Interest:

Lake Vyrnwy. This is now a reservoir serving Liverpool's water needs. The lake is 4 ¾ miles long and about a third of a mile broad on average. The start of the construction of the reservoir was in 1880, the foundation stone being laid by the Third Earl of Powis in 1881. At the north-east end, the dam is tied into rock but on the south-west into the clay of the hill. The roadway over the dam is carried by 33 arches through which the water flows. The area of the lake when full is 1,121 acres and at its deepest, 84ft. The setting amid hills over 2,000 ft in height and the maturity now of the trees (mainly conifers) planted on the side of the valley have taken the 'manmadeness' and starkness from the scene making it in many ways as attractive as any Italian or alpine lake.

Llanwddyn (meaning 'clean, pretty and lovely place') In earlier times on Good Friday, Christmas and St. John's day, the people of this valley competed in throwing a large rock weighing 75 pounds. The record distance thrown was 15 yards. The stone may be seen in the church. Other quaint past-times included a football match in which 150 players took part by moonlight!

Accommodation:

H. A. Parry, Tynymaes, *Llanwddyn*, SY10 0NN (069173) 216
1 D, 2 T, EM, C.

Mrs. M. Jones, Fronheulog, *Llanwddyn*, SY10 0NN (069173) 662
2 D, 1 S, EM, C, V.

Lake Vyrnwy Hotel, *Llanwddyn*, SY10 0LY. (069173) 692. All types of accommodation available. EM, Dg, (By arrangement).

1. From the Cann Office Hotel at Llangadfan, go left along the main A458 road then right along the B4395 (north), for 1 mile.

2. Take 1st lane on your left and follow this to the point where a path goes north (right) along the side of a field and between trees. You now enter Dyfnant Forest.

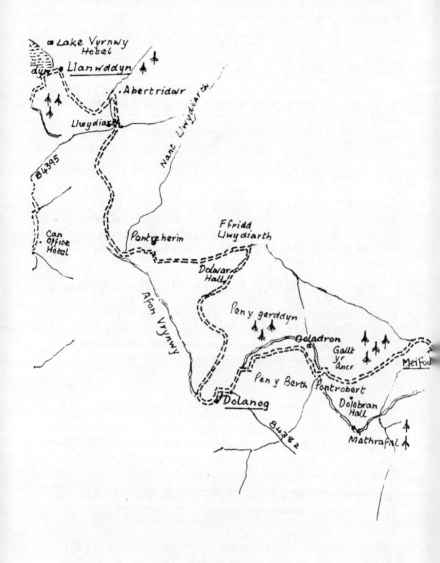

SECTIONS 14 & 15: 14. Llanwddyn — Dolanog
15. Dolanog – Meifod

56

3. In less than half a mile you enter a forest road. Turn left along this. This is where you will need to consult the map and compass and the aim is to reach a footbridge crossing a stream to Hendre Dyfnant (not named on 1:50000 Map) but at GR 000115. Pass Hendre Dyfnant and turn right (east) at the lane junction. Follow this forest track to the road at Ddol Conway, heading north-north-east from Hendre Dyfnant and through the forestry along the track.

4. At the road at Ddol Conway, turn left onto lane and then right along a track which leaves the road at an angle.

5. A short way along here, as you approach Bryn Conwy, you bear right, ascending.

6. As there is a junction in the paths you can take either course because they join each other again and you should arrive at the forest edge and the visitors centre and Lake Vyrnwy. (About 1 mile from Bryn Conwy).

7. Take the road across the dam, turn right and enter Llanwddyn.

Lake Vyrnwy

14. Llanwddyn — Dolanog

Distance: 10 miles/16km

Terrain: Good roads and tracks with some forestry tracks

Time: 3½ hours

Map: O.S. 1:50000. Sheet 125 (Bala & Lake Vyrnwy)

Points of Interest:

Dolwar Hall. A good example of cruck framed architecture.

Dolwar Fach Farm. Once the home of Ann Griffiths a famous Welsh hymn writer in the latter part of the 18th C. who composed only in Welsh.

Allt Dolanog — Iron Age hill fort.

Accommodation:

Mr. & Mrs. G. E. Jenkins, Cyfie Farm (See Sketch Map), Llanfihangel, *Llanfyllin*, SY22 5JE (069184) 451
1 T, 1 D/T, 1 F, EM, V.

Mrs. Llinos Jones, Gadair Farm, *Llanfyllin*, SY22 5LD (069184) 271
1 D/T, 1 S, 1 F, EM, V, Dg.

1. From Llanwddyn take the B4393 road for Llanfyllin. Pass the turn for Cwm Hirnant but do not take this. Instead continue in a southerly direction until about half a mile you reach a sharp hairpin bend. Here, turn right and enter a minor lane which leads directly south at first, then veers south-west.

2. Continue along this lane for about a mile to a point where there is a forestry road leading left. This climbs into the forest and you follow it first up, then down all the way to Llywdiarth (1½ miles).

3. At Llywdiarth and *before* crossing Pont Llogel (Bridge), turn left and follow the course of Afon Vyrnwy, passing a Forestry Commission picnic area along this stretch.

4. Follow the river until it meets Nant Llywdiarth, a stream. There, cross stream and bear left up and away from the valley crossing several steep pastures and a minor road and eventually entering a farm track.

5. Pass this farm, cross a hill and descend after about half a mile to a farm at Pentre Herin and a minor road.

6. Here, turn right and follow the road descending for less than half a mile to a long right hand bend.

7. Take the track which leads off to the left and follow this for about a mile to the 'T' junction with the B4382.

8. At junction on B4382 turn right and in about half a mile you will pass by Dolwar Hall. Continue along the B4382 for another half a mile passing Dolwar Fach on your right.

9. Just beyond the track to Dolwar Fach, the Way leaves the road and goes south (left) and you climb the hill of Allt Dolanog and contour around the eastern side to reach a lane.

10. At the lane, turn right and follow this to Dolanog (half a mile).

15. Dolanog — Meifod

Distance: 6 miles/10km

Terrain: Apart from one rather steep descent, pleasant section of roads and good tracks

Time: 3 hours

Map: O.S. 1:50000. Sheet 125 (Bala & Lake Vyrnwy)

Points of Interest:

Felin Dolanog. A mill used for the cleaning and bleaching of Welsh flannel.

Pont Robert (Robert's Bridge) named after Oliver ap Robert who built the bridge over the river in 1670.

Dolobran Hall. Built by Charles Lloyd in 1657 and an ancester of the founder of Lloyds Bank. Charles Lloyd was a Quaker and worshipped in a nearby old Quaker Meeting House. In 1662 a meeting was interrupted and several people were arrested, including Lloyd. His estates were confiscated and the house demolished. He was imprisoned in Welshpool gaol and died there 10 years later.

Gallt yr Ancr. ('Hill of the anchorite') so named because of St. Gwyddfach, who came from Brittany with a band of Christian missionaries early in the 6th C. and who lived as a hermit on this hill.

Meifod. ('Lowland campaign dwelling') The church is the most recent of three built here and is in the Norman style dedicated to St. Mary and consecrated in 1155. By the font is an inscribed stone thought to be a monument to Madoc ap Maredudd, Prince of Powys, who was buried at Meifod but it is also said to be the original monument to St. Gwyddfach.

Accommodation:

Audrey Pryce, Prenrhwnin, Trefnanney, *Meifod* (069181) 632
1 T, 1 D, 1 S, EM (By arrangement) V. Own lounge/tea-making facilities.

Mrs. S. M. Watkin, Pentrego, *Meifod*, Powys. SY22 6DH (093884) 353
T, D and Single available, EM, Camp, V, Dg.

1. Leave Dolanog by taking the B4382, crossing the old stone bridge over Afon Vyrnwy. (The man made weir years ago drove a water wheel for the grain and fulling mill, Felin Dolanog).

2. Immediately, turn left and follow the course of the river heading in a north-easterly direction with the river on your left and skirting the steep banks of Pen-y-Berth on your right.

3. The path gradually winds in an easterly direction, still following the river, passing between the two steep hills. (Allt Dolanog and Pen y Berth). Keep close to the river in this steeply-sided section until you enter a lane which still runs parallel to the river banks.

4. Continue along this lane and pass Dolodron Farm (you are now heading south south-east) to join the minor road and continue in same direction for half a mile until you reach a T junction where turn left and enter the village of Pontrobert.

5. Here, go over the bridge (Oliver ap Robert's bridge) and take first lane right. After the last chapel, take the lane bearing right (east) and go along this and the track passing to the north of Dolobran Hall.

6. After Dolobran Hall, you join a lane which leads onto a minor road.

7. At the minor road, turn right and after a short while, take the path which leads up and left and in a north-easterly direction flanking Gallt yr Ancr.

8. Descend north-east through Dyffryn Hall Wood to reach the road where turn right and enter Meifod.

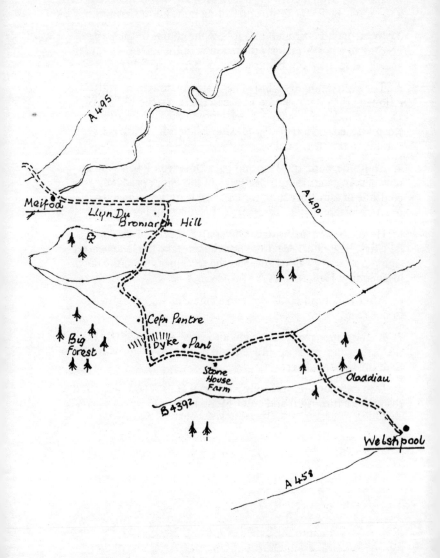

SECTION 16:   Meifod — Welshpool

16. Meifod — Welshpool

Distance: 10 miles/16km

Terrain: Steep at start of this section with some main road then more steeply if you join Offa's Dyke path at Hope

Time: 5 hours

Maps: O.S. 1:50000 Sheet 125 (Bala & Lake Vyrnwy) Sheet 126 (Shrewsbury)

Points of Interest:

Fronlas. An ancient fortification.

Cefn Pentre. To the west of this farm lies an Iron Age fort.

Bwlch Aedded. Near this farm is an earth-work of the same name which was probably the outer defence link of Mathrafal Palace the home of the Princes of Powys from the latter half of the 8th C. and where they remained until the 12th C. It then fell into the hands of Robert Vipont, a baron and a favourite of English King John who rebuilt and fortified the Palace. After rebuilding and fortifying and disputes between Vipont and Llewellyn ap Iorweth (Prince of North Wales) King John sent his troops from England to oust Llewellyn, razed the castle to the ground and it was never rebuilt. A farmhouse now stands nearby.

Welshpool (Trallwng). A mainly Georgian town but with some older buildings. The church is dedicated to St. Mary the Virgin and there have been several additions. The panelled roof is said to have been taken from the Abbey at Strata Marcella.

Light Railway. One of Wales's lovely little narrow gauge railways which runs from Welshpool 9 miles up the valley to Llanfair Caereinion.

Powis Castle. A mile and a half outside the town on the Newtown Road originally in the hands of Welsh Royalty and changed hands several times during the residence of the Princes of Powys. Came into the hands of Edward Herbert in Elizabethan era, a descendant of Gwenwynwyn, one of the original occupants and a governor of Powys around 1149. Fell to Cromwell in the Civil War but was not damaged. Open to the public. National Trust. Superb grounds and gardens.

Accommodation:

Mrs. Freda Emberton, Tynllwyn Farm, *Welshpool* SY21 9BW
(0938) 553175/553054
2 D, 2 T, 2 F, S (at small supp) EM, Camp, V, Dg, (By
arrangement)

Gwyneth Jones, Moat Farm, *Welshpool* SY21 8SE (0938) 553179
1 T, 1 D, 1 F, EM, V.

The Royal Oak Hotel, The Cross, *Welshpool* SY21 7DG (0938)
552217
All types of rooms, EM, V.

Mrs. F. M. Hughes, Plasdwpa, *Berriew*, *Welshpool* (068685)
298 (Off route).
Various rooms, EM, Camp, Dg (By arrangement).

1. Passing between two chapels in Meifod, head south-east
across Afon Vyrnwy.

2. At Y Junction turn left and after a quarter of a mile, take the
footpath right (east) which climbs up through forestry.

3. On coming out of the trees, you will find that your path is
above Llyn Du (the Black Lake).

4. Still continuing in this easterly direction for a short while
after your view of the lake, you will reach a road. (This passes
woodland in which there is the fortification at Bronlas).

5. At road, turn right and continue along the road, crossing the
cross-roads and carrying straight on in a south-easterly direction
for about a mile.

6. At the next junction, turn right and look for a path leading
off the lane immediately left and take this.

7. Follow this in a south south-easterly direction to the farm at
Cefn Pentre. (To the west of this is the site of an Iron Age fort).
Also, the public footpath of this section is in some doubt.

8. Cross the minor road and continue across fields in a southerly
direction until you reach some woodland.

9. At this deciduous wood, (Bwlch Clump) the path turns right
along-side the woodland. (To the east of this wood is the farm
Bwlch Aedded below which is the earth work).

10. You will reach a lane and still continuing in the same
direction, (south) take this lane and go down-hill for about an
eighth of a mile where turn left (east) into a field.

11. Cross field down to and across a stream and onto caravan park ahead of you at Pant.

12. From the caravan park, continue in an easterly direction to shortly reach the B4392 where turn left along this.

13. Proceed along the B4392 for about ½ a mile, taking the first turning on your right into a minor lane and heading in a south, south-easterly direction.

14. Follow this lane to the cross-roads.

15. At cross-roads, continue straight across and in the same south easterly direction and in about a mile you enter Welshpool — 'the Way' has been completed.

Welshpool

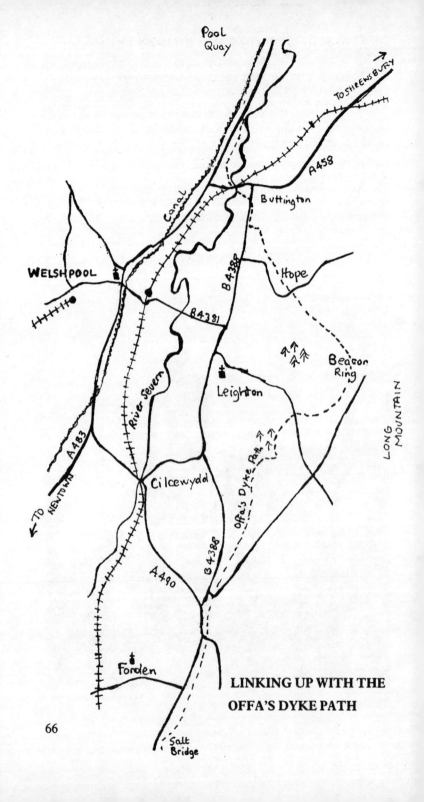

LINKING UP WITH THE
OFFA'S DYKE PATH

66

Linking up with the Offa's Dyke Path

For those wishing to complete a circular walk, follow Offa's Dyke long distance footpath from Welshpool to Knighton.

Join Offa's Dyke Path by walking along the B4381 to Lower Leighton T junction. Here, turn left along the B4388 then take the next turning right along Hope Lane to the Village of Hope. Go past 'Corner House', climb steeply and just past a road on the right is a signpost for the Offa's Dyke footpath. The journey from Hope to Knighton is about 26 miles.

To join Offa's Dyke Path from Powis Castle, head south along the A483 (towards Newtown) and take the A490 to Cilcewydd to the junction of the A490 and B4388. The latter road south from here is part of the Offa's Dyke Path. The journey from the junction of the A490 and B4388 is about 22 miles.

The first part of the route is flat but through some lovely Montgomeryshire farmland. The end section (beyond Churchstoke) as it approaches Knighton offers stupendous wide views of England & Wales and follows the actual old earth-works of the Dyke itself for many miles.

Details and route maps can be obtained from the Offa's Dyke Association (see 'Useful Addresses' section).

Owain Glyndŵr's Coat of Arms

GLOSSARY OF WORDS AND PLACE NAMES

Aber	River mouth
Afon	River
Allt	Wooded hill
Bach/Fach	Small
Blaen	Head of valley
Bron	Slope, brow of hill
Bryn	Hill
Bwlch	Pass/gap
Braich/Trum	Ridge/Spur
Caer/Gaer	Hill Fort
Carreg	Stone
Castell	Castle
Carn/Garn	Cairn or pile of stones
Coed	Wood
Craig	Rocky outcrop or cliff
Cors/Gors	Bog
Cefn	Back/Ridge
Clawdd	Ditch/Dyke
Crug	Hillock
Cwm	Valley
Ddu/Du	Black
Dan/Tan	Under
Eglwys	Church
Esgair	Ridge
Fan	Peak/Top
Fawr/Mawr	Large
Ffordd	Road
Foel/Moel	Bare hill
Ffridd	Mountain pasture
Ffynnon	Springs
Garn/Gron	Rounded cairn
Gelli/Celli	Grove/Copse
Glan	River
Glas/Las	Blue
Gwyn/Gwen	White
Gwaelod	Foot of hill
Glan/Lan	River bank
Hafod	Summer dwelling
Hendre	Winter dwelling
Hir	Long
Is	Below or Under

Isaf	Lower
Llan	Church
Llethr	Slope
Llyn	Lake
Llwybr	Path
Llwyd/Lwyd	Grey
Maes	Meadow/Field
Maen	Standing stone
Mynydd	Mountain
Melyn/Felyn	Colour yellow
Melin/Felin	Mill
Nant	Brook
Neuadd	Mansion/Hall
Ogof	Cave
Pandy	Fulling mill
Pant	Hollow valley
Pen	Peak or top
Pentre	Village
Plas	Mansion
Pont/Bont	Bridge
Pwll/Bwll	Pool
Rhiw	Hillside
Rhos	Moorland
Rhaeadr	Waterfall
Rhyd	Ford
Tomen	Mound
Ty	House
Troed	Foot
Sarn	Causeway
Waun	Moorland
Wern (Gwaun)	Bog/Marshland
Ystrad	Wide valley bottom/Valley floor

ACKNOWLEDGEMENTS AND FURTHER READING

Our thanks go to the Curator of the Owain Glyndŵr Museum, Machynlleth and the Local History Section of Shropshire Libraries, Shrewsbury, for valuable assistance.

Ancient Stones of Wales: C Barber & J G Williams
Blorenge Books 1989

Battle of Shrewsbury 1403: E J Priestley
Shrewsbury & Atcham Borough Council 1979

Historical Atlas of Wales : W Rees
Faber & Faber 1959

In Search of Birds in Mid-Wales : B O'Shea & J Green
Artery Publications 1988

Matter of Wales: J Morris
Penguin 1987

Mid-Wales Companion : M K Stone
A Nelson 1989

More Mysterious Wales : C Barber
Paladin Grafton 1983

Mysterious Wales : C Barber
Paladin Grafton 1983

Nature of Central Wales : F Slater (Editor)
Barracuda Books 1988

Offa's Dyke Path (2 vols.) 1. Sedbury to Knighton; 2. Knighton to Prestatyn: K & E Kay & M Richards
Ordnance Survey & Aurum Press 1989

Owain Glyndŵr : G A Jones
University of Wales Press, Cardiff

Owain Glyndŵr — Prince of Wales : I Skidmore
Christopher Davies 1986

Owain Glyndŵr's Way : R Sale
Hutchinson 1985 (Out of Print)

Powys Montgomeryshire Village Book : Federation of Women's Institutes
Countryside Books 1989

Wales in the Early Middle Ages : W Davies
Leicester University Press 1982

Welsh Place Names : J Jones
John Jones Publishing 1988

Where to Watch Birds in Wales : D Saunders
C. Helm 1987

Owain Glyndŵr : Tywysog Cymru, Prince of Wales, Parliament
House, Machynlleth

---

*The Publishers of this guide also publish 'Best Walks in the
Shropshire Hills' by Gillian Walker, 'Henley, the Best
Organised Picnic in Europe' by James Turner and a wide
range of business and management books and directories
dealing with jobs, finance, investment, management techniques
and skills, marketing, training films, etc.*

*We also publish a series of high quality photographs of
Shrewsbury, Chester and Ludlow available from local
stockists including Tourist Information Centres, Museums,
etc. Further details available on request.*
